MW01001096

The Prayer MAP® for a LESS STRESSED LIFE

BARBOUR
PUBLISHING

Scripture quotations marked MSG are from *THE MESSAGE*. Copyright © by Eugene H. Peterson 1993, 1994, 1995, 1996, 2000, 2001, 2002. Used by permission of NavPress Publishing Group.

Scripture quotations marked NLT are taken from the *Holy Bible*. New Living Translation copyright© 1996, 2004, 2015 by Tyndale House Foundation. Used by permission of Tyndale House Publishers, Inc. Carol Stream, Illinois 60188. All rights reserved.

Scripture quotations marked ESV are from The Holy Bible, English Standard Version®, copyright © 2001 by Crossway Bibles, a publishing ministry of Good News Publishers. Used by permission. All rights reserved.

Scripture quotations marked AMP are taken from the Amplified® Bible, © 2015 by The Lockman Foundation. Used by permission.

Scripture quotations marked AMPC are taken from the Amplified® Bible, Classic Edition © 1954, 1958, 1962, 1964, 1965, 1987 by The Lockman Foundation. Used by permission.

Scripture quotations marked GW are taken from GOD'S WORD®, © 1995 God's Word to the Nations. Used by permission of God's Word Mission Society.

Scripture quotations marked PHILLIPS are taken from The New Testament in Modern English by J. B. Phillips copyright © 1960, 1972 J. B. Phillips. Administered by The Archbishops' Council of the Church of England. Used by Permission.

Published by Barbour Books, an imprint of Barbour Publishing, Inc., 1810 Barbour Drive, Uhrichsville, Ohio 44683, www.barbourbooks.com

Our mission is to inspire the world with the life-changing message of the Bible.

Printed in China.

What Does a LESS STRESSED LIFE Look Like? . . .

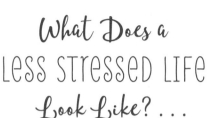

Get ready to experience the delightful freedom of stress-free living with this creative journal, where every colorful page will guide you to create your very own stress-reducing prayer map—as you write out specific thoughts, ideas, and lists, which you can follow (from start to finish!)—as you talk to God. (Be sure to record the date on each one of your prayer maps so you can look back over time and see how God has continued to work in your life!)

The Prayer Map for a Less Stressed Life will not only encourage you to spend time talking with God and letting go of those things that cause you to feel tension and anxiety. . .it will also help you build a healthy spiritual habit of continual prayer for life!

DATE:

Dear Heavenly Father,

Today I am stressed because...

....
....
....
....
.... (and I'm giving it all to you!)

I'm feeling...

....
....
....
....

I need your help focusing my thoughts on...

....
....
....

instead of ....

....
....
....

I need Your guidance with. . .

....

....

....

....

....

Help me to be thankful for all of life's blessings (big and small!), including. . .

....

....

....

....

....

Thank You, Father, for hearing my prayers. Amen.

"Give in to God, come to terms with him and everything will turn out just fine. Let him tell you what to do; take his words to heart."

JOB 22:21–22 MSG

DATE:

Dear Heavenly Father,

Today I am stressed because...

....

....

....

....

.... (and I'm giving it all to you!)

I'm feeling...

....

....

....

....

I need your help focusing my thoughts on...

....

....

instead of ....

....

....

....

I need Your guidance with. . .

....

....

....

....

....

....

Help me to be thankful for all of life's
blessings (big and small!), including. . .

....

....

....

....

....

Thank You, Father, for hearing my prayers. Amen.

*Trust GOD from the bottom of your heart; don't
try to figure out everything on your own. Listen for
GOD's voice in everything you do, everywhere you go;
he's the one who will keep you on track.*

PROVERBS 3:5–6 MSG

DATE:

Dear Heavenly Father,

TODAY I AM STRESSED BECAUSE...

....
....
....
....
.... (AND I'M GIVING IT ALL TO YOU!)

I'm feeling...

....
....
....
....

I NEED YOUR HELP FOCUSING MY THOUGHTS ON...

....
....

INSTEAD OF ....

....
....
....

I need Your guidance with...

....

....

....

....

....

Help me to be thankful for all of life's blessings (big and small!), including...

....

....

....

....

....

Thank You, Father, for hearing my prayers. Amen.

> *I'm not trying to win the approval of people, but of God. If pleasing people were my goal, I would not be Christ's servant.*
>
> GALATIANS 1:10 NLT

DATE:

Dear Heavenly Father,

Today I am stressed because...

....

....

....

....

.... (and I'm giving it all to you!)

I'm feeling...

....

....

....

....

I need your help focusing my thoughts on...

....

....

....

instead of ....

....

....

....

I need Your guidance with. . .

....

....

....

....

....

Help me to be thankful for all of life's blessings (big and small), including. . .

....

....

....

....

....

Thank You, Father, for hearing my prayers. Amen.

*When troubles of any kind come your way,
consider it an opportunity for great joy.*

JAMES 1:2 NLT

DATE:

Dear Heavenly Father,

Today I am stressed because...

....
....
....
....
.... (and I'm giving it all to you!)

I'm feeling...

....
....
....
....

I need your help focusing my thoughts on...

....
....
....

instead of ....
....
....
....

I need Your guidance with. . .

....

....

....

....

....

....

Help me to be thankful for all of life's blessings (big and small!), including. . .

....

....

....

....

....

Thank You, Father, for hearing my prayers. Amen.

I press on to reach the end of the race and receive the heavenly prize for which God, through Christ Jesus, is calling us.

PHILIPPIANS 3:14 NLT

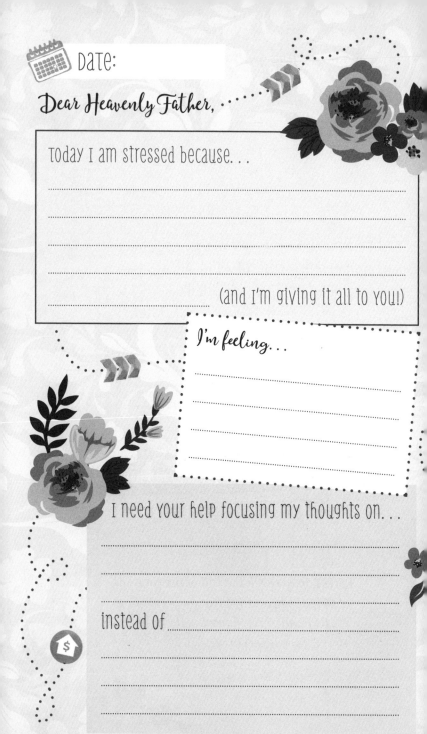

Date:

Dear Heavenly Father,

Today I am stressed because...

....

....

....

....

.... (and I'm giving it all to You!)

I'm feeling...

....

....

....

....

I need Your help focusing my thoughts on...

....

....

....

Instead of ....

....

....

....

I need Your guidance with. . .

....

....

....

....

....

....

Help me to be thankful for all of life's blessings (big and small), including. . .

....

....

....

....

....

Thank You, Father, for hearing my prayers. Amen.

We do not know what to do,
but our eyes are upon You.
2 CHRONICLES 20:12 AMPC

Date:

Dear Heavenly Father,

Today I am stressed because. . .

....

....

....

....

.... (and I'm giving it all to you!)

I'm feeling. . .

....

....

....

....

I need your help focusing my thoughts on. . .

....

....

....

Instead of ....

....

....

....

I need Your guidance with. . .

....

....

....

....

....

....

Help me to be thankful for all of life's blessings (big and small!), including. . .

....

....

....

....

....

Thank You, Father, for hearing my prayers. Amen.

If you abide in My word [hold fast to My teachings and live in accordance with them], you are truly My disciples. And you will know the Truth, and the Truth will set you free.

JOHN 8:31–32 AMPC

DATE:

Dear Heavenly Father,

TODAY I am stressed because. . .

....

....

....

....

.... (and I'm giving it all to you!)

I'm feeling. . .

....

....

....

....

I need your help focusing my thoughts on. . .

....

....

....

instead of ....

....

....

....

I need Your guidance with. . .

....

....

....

....

....

Help me to be thankful for all of life's
blessings (big and small!), including. . .

....

....

....

....

....

Thank You, Father, for hearing my prayers. Amen.

*[It is] the Spirit of God that made me [which has
stirred me up], and the breath of the Almighty
that gives me life [which inspires me].*

JOB 33:4 AMPC

DATE:

Dear Heavenly Father,

Today I am stressed because...

....

....

....

....

.... (and I'm giving it all to you!)

I'm feeling...

....

....

....

....

I need your help focusing my thoughts on...

....

....

....

instead of ....

....

....

....

I need Your guidance with. . .

....

....

....

....

....

....

Help me to be thankful for all of life's blessings (big and small!), including. . .

....

....

....

....

....

Thank You, Father, for hearing my prayers. Amen.

The LORD is my light and my salvation.
Who is there to fear?
PSALM 27:1 GW

DATE:

Dear Heavenly Father,

Today I am stressed because...

....

....

....

....

.... (and I'm giving it all to You!)

I'm feeling...

....

....

....

....

I need Your help focusing my thoughts on...

....

....

....

instead of ....

....

....

I need Your guidance with. . .

....

....

....

....

....

Help me to be thankful for all of life's blessings (big and small!), including. . .

....

....

....

....

Thank You, Father, for hearing my prayers. Amen.

The Lord is the Refuge and Stronghold of my life. . . .
Though a host encamp against me, my heart shall
not fear; though war arise against me,
[even then] in this will I be confident.
PSALM 27:1, 3 AMPC

Date:

Dear Heavenly Father,

Today I am stressed because. . .

....

....

....

....

.... (and I'm giving it all to you!)

I'm feeling. . .

....

....

....

....

I need your help focusing my thoughts on. . .

....

....

....

instead of ....

....

....

....

I need Your guidance with...

....

....

....

....

....

....

Help me to be thankful for all of life's blessings (big and small!), including...

....

....

....

....

....

Thank You, Father, for hearing my prayers. Amen.

*He will give His angels [especial] charge over you
to accompany and defend and preserve you in
all your ways [of obedience and service].
They shall bear you up on their hands.*
PSALM 91:11–12 AMPC

Date:

Dear Heavenly Father,

Today I am stressed because. . .

....

....

....

....

.... (and I'm giving it all to you!)

I'm feeling. . .

....

....

....

....

I need your help focusing my thoughts on. . .

....

....

Instead of ....

....

....

....

I need Your guidance with. . .

....

....

....

....

....

....

Help me to be thankful for all of life's blessings (big and small!), including. . .

....

....

....

....

....

Thank You, Father, for hearing my prayers. Amen.

"Oh, how my soul praises the Lord.
How my spirit rejoices in God my Savior!"
LUKE 1:46–47 NLT

DATE:

Dear Heavenly Father,

Today I am stressed because...

....
....
....
....
.... (and I'm giving it all to you!)

I'm feeling...

....
....
....
....

I need your help focusing my thoughts on...

....
....
....
instead of ....
....
....
....

I need Your guidance with. . .

....

....

....

....

....

....

Help me to be thankful for all of life's blessings (big and small!), including. . .

....

....

....

....

....

Thank You, Father, for hearing my prayers. Amen.

"You will see neither wind nor rain. . .
but this valley will be filled with water. You will
have plenty. . . . But this is only a simple thing for
the LORD, for he will make you victorious."
2 KINGS 3:16–18 NLT

DATE:

Dear Heavenly Father,

Today I am stressed because...

....
....
....
....
.... (and I'm giving it all to You!)

I'm feeling...

....
....
....
....

I need Your help focusing my thoughts on...

....
....
....

instead of ....
....
....
....

I need Your guidance with...

....

....

....

....

....

Help me to be thankful for all of life's blessings (big and small!), including...

....

....

....

....

....

Thank You, Father, for hearing my prayers. Amen.

*Commit your actions to the LORD,
and your plans will succeed.*
PROVERBS 16:3 NLT

Dear Heavenly Father,

Today I am stressed because. . .

....
....
....
....
.... (and I'm giving it all to you!)

I'm feeling. . .

....
....
....
....

I need your help focusing my thoughts on. . .

....
....
....

instead of ....
....
....
....

I need Your guidance with. . .

....

....

....

....

....

Help me to be thankful for all of life's
blessings (big and small!), including. . .

....

....

....

....

....

Thank You, Father, for hearing my prayers. Amen.

*The minute I said, "I'm slipping, I'm falling,"
your love, GOD, took hold and held me fast.
When I was upset and beside myself, you
calmed me down and cheered me up.*
PSALM 94:18–19 MSG

DATE:

Dear Heavenly Father,

Today I am stressed because. . .

....

....

....

....

.... (and I'm giving it all to You!)

I'm feeling. . .

....

....

....

....

I need Your help focusing my thoughts on. . .

....

....

....

instead of ....

....

....

....

I need Your guidance with. . .

....

....

....

....

....

Help me to be thankful for all of life's blessings (big and small!), including. . .

....

....

....

....

....

Thank You, Father, for hearing my prayers. Amen.

A cheerful disposition is good for your health;
gloom and doom leave you bone-tired.
PROVERBS 17:22 MSG

date:

Dear Heavenly Father,

Today I am stressed because. . .

....

....

....

....

.... (and I'm giving it all to you!)

I'm feeling. . .

....

....

....

....

I need your help focusing my thoughts on. . .

....

....

....

instead of ....

....

....

....

I need Your guidance with. . .

....
....
....
....
....
....

Help me to be thankful for all of life's blessings (big and small!), including. . .

....
....
....
....
....

Thank You, Father, for hearing my prayers. Amen.

For God is not a God of disorder but of peace.
1 CORINTHIANS 14:33 NLT

DATE:

Dear Heavenly Father, ·····

TODAY I am stressed because...

....

....

....

....

.... (and I'm giving it all to you!)

I'm feeling...

....

....

....

....

I need your help focusing my thoughts on...

....

....

....

instead of ....

....

....

....

I need Your guidance with. . .

....

....

....

....

....

Help me to be thankful for all of life's blessings (big and small!), including. . .

....

....

....

....

Thank You, Father, for hearing my prayers. Amen.

*Let us also lay aside every weight. . .looking to Jesus,
the founder and perfecter of our faith.*
HEBREWS 12:1–2 ESV

DATE:

Dear Heavenly Father,

Today I am stressed because...

....

....

....

....

.... (and I'm giving it all to You!)

I'm feeling...

....

....

....

I need Your help focusing my thoughts on...

....

....

....

instead of ....

....

....

....

I need Your guidance with. . .

....

....

....

....

....

....

Help me to be thankful for all of life's blessings (big and small!), including. . .

....

....

....

....

Thank You, Father, for hearing my prayers. Amen.

"When someone gives you a hard time, respond with the energies of prayer, for then you are working out of your true selves, your God-created selves."
MATTHEW 5:44–45 MSG

Date:

Dear Heavenly Father,

Today I am stressed because. . .

....

....

....

....

.... (and I'm giving it all to you!)

I'm feeling. . .

....

....

....

....

I need your help focusing my thoughts on. . .

....

....

....

instead of ....

....

....

....

I need Your guidance with. . .

....

....

....

....

....

Help me to be thankful for all of life's blessings (big and small!), including. . .

....

....

....

....

....

Thank You, Father, for hearing my prayers. Amen.

Why are you in despair, O my soul? And why have you become restless and disturbed within me? Hope in God and wait expectantly for Him, for I shall again praise Him for the help of His presence.

PSALM 42:5 AMP

DATE:

Dear Heavenly Father,

today I am stressed because...

....
....
....
....
.... (and I'm giving it all to you!)

I'm feeling...

....
....
....
....

I need your help focusing my thoughts on...

....
....
....

instead of ....

....
....
....

I need Your guidance with...

....

....

....

....

....

Help me to be thankful for all of life's blessings (big and small!), including. . .

....

....

....

....

....

Thank You, Father, for hearing my prayers. Amen.

The Scriptures give us hope and encouragement as we wait patiently for God's promises to be fulfilled.
ROMANS 15:4 NLT

DATE:

Dear Heavenly Father,

Today I am stressed because. . .

....

....

....

....

.... (and I'm giving it all to you!)

I'm feeling. . .

....

....

....

....

I need your help focusing my thoughts on. . .

....

....

....

instead of ....

....

....

I need Your guidance with. . .

....

....

....

....

....

....

Help me to be thankful for all of life's blessings (big and small!), including. . .

....

....

....

....

....

Thank You, Father, for hearing my prayers. Amen.

Stand by the roads and look; and ask for the eternal paths, where the good, old way is; then walk in it, and you will find rest for your souls.
JEREMIAH 6:16 AMPC

Date:

Dear Heavenly Father,

Today I am stressed because...

....
....
....
....
.... (and I'm giving it all to you!)

I'm feeling...

....
....
....
....

I need your help focusing my thoughts on...

....
....
....

instead of ....

....
....
....

I need Your guidance with...

....

....

....

....

....

Help me to be thankful for all of life's blessings (big and small!), including...

....

....

....

....

....

Thank You, Father, for hearing my prayers. Amen.

*"People judge by outward appearance,
but the LORD looks at the heart."*
1 SAMUEL 16:7 NLT

Date:

Dear Heavenly Father,

Today I am stressed because...

....

....

....

.... (and I'm giving it all to you!)

I'm feeling...

....

....

....

I need your help focusing my thoughts on...

....

....

instead of ....

....

....

I need Your guidance with. . .

....

....

....

....

....

Help me to be thankful for all of life's blessings (big and small!), including. . .

....

....

....

....

Thank You, Father, for hearing my prayers. Amen.

Then you will seek Me, inquire for, and require Me [as a vital necessity] and find Me when you search for Me with all your heart.

JEREMIAH 29:13 AMPC

DATE:

Dear Heavenly Father,

Today I am stressed because...

....
....
....
....
.... (and I'm giving it all to You!)

I'm feeling...

....
....
....
....

I need Your help focusing my thoughts on...

....
....
....

instead of..
....
....
....

I need Your guidance with. . .

....

....

....

....

....

Help me to be thankful for all of life's blessings (big and small), including. . .

....

....

....

....

Thank You, Father, for hearing my prayers. Amen.

Let the words of my mouth and the meditation of my heart be acceptable in Your sight, O Lord, my [firm, impenetrable] Rock and my Redeemer.

PSALM 19:14 AMPC

Date: _____

Dear Heavenly Father,

Today I am stressed because. . .

....
....
....
....
.... (and I'm giving it all to You!)

I'm feeling. . .

....
....
....
....

I need Your help focusing my thoughts on. . .

....
....
....

Instead of ....
....
....
....

I need Your guidance with. . .

....
....
....
....
....
....

Help me to be thankful for all of life's blessings (big and small!), including. . .

....
....
....
....
....

Thank You, Father, for hearing my prayers. Amen.

Fix your thoughts on what is true, and honorable, and right, and pure, and lovely, and admirable. Think about things that are excellent and worthy of praise.
PHILIPPIANS 4:8 NLT

Date:

Dear Heavenly Father,

today I am stressed because. . .

....
....
....
....
.... (and I'm giving it all to you!)

I'm feeling. . .

....
....
....
....

I need your help focusing my thoughts on. . .

....
....
....
instead of ....
....
....
....

I need Your guidance with...

....
....
....
....
....
....

Help me to be thankful for all of life's
blessings (big and small!), including...

....
....
....
....

Thank You, Father, for hearing my prayers. Amen.

*"As it is written in the Scriptures, 'They will all be
taught by God.' Everyone who listens to the Father
and learns from him comes to me."*

JOHN 6:45 NLT

Date:

Dear Heavenly Father,

Today I am stressed because. . .

....

....

....

....

.... (and I'm giving it all to you!)

I'm feeling. . .

....

....

....

....

I need your help focusing my thoughts on. . .

....

....

instead of ....

....

....

I need Your guidance with. . .

....
....
....
....
....
....

Help me to be thankful for all of life's blessings (big and small!), including. . .

....
....
....
....

Thank You, Father, for hearing my prayers. Amen.

Right behind you a voice will say, "This is the way you should go," whether to the right or to the left.
ISAIAH 30:21 NLT

DATE:

Dear Heavenly Father,

Today I am stressed because. . .

....

....

....

.... (and I'm giving it all to you!)

I'm feeling. . .

....

....

....

....

I need your help focusing my thoughts on. . .

....

....

....

instead of ....

....

....

....

I need Your guidance with. . .

....

....

....

....

....

Help me to be thankful for all of life's blessings (big and small), including. . .

....

....

....

....

....

Thank You, Father, for hearing my prayers. Amen.

God is our refuge and strength, a very present help in trouble. Therefore we will not fear though the earth gives way, though the mountains be moved into the heart of the sea.
PSALM 46:1–2 ESV

Date:

Dear Heavenly Father,

Today I am stressed because. . .

....

....

....

....

.... (and I'm giving it all to you!)

I'm feeling. . .

....

....

....

....

I need your help focusing my thoughts on. . .

....

....

....

instead of ....

....

....

....

I need Your guidance with. . .

....

....

....

....

....

....

Help me to be thankful for all of life's
blessings (big and small!), including. . .

....

....

....

....

....

Thank You, Father, for hearing my prayers. Amen.

"Incline your ear, O LORD, and hear;
open your eyes, O LORD, and see."
2 KINGS 19:16 ESV

DATE:

Dear Heavenly Father,

today I am stressed because...

....

....

....

....

.... (and I'm giving it all to you!)

I'm feeling...

....

....

....

....

I need your help focusing my thoughts on...

....

....

....

instead of ....

....

....

....

I need Your guidance with. . .

....

....

....

....

....

Help me to be thankful for all of life's blessings (big and small!), including. . .

....

....

....

....

....

Thank You, Father, for hearing my prayers. Amen.

He will feed his flock like a shepherd. He will carry the lambs in his arms, holding them close to his heart.

ISAIAH 40:11 NLT

DATE:

Dear Heavenly Father,

Today I am stressed because...

....
....
....
....
.... (and I'm giving it all to you!)

I'm feeling...

....
....
....
....

I need your help focusing my thoughts on...

....
....
....

instead of ....

....
....
....

I need Your guidance with. . .

_____

_____

_____

_____

_____

_____

Help me to be thankful for all of life's blessings (big and small!), including. . .

_____

_____

_____

_____

_____

Thank You, Father, for hearing my prayers. Amen.

_The LORD replied, "I will personally go with you. . .and I
will give you rest—everything will be fine for you."_
EXODUS 33:14 NLT

Date:

Dear Heavenly Father,

Today I am stressed because. . .

....
....
....
....
.... (and I'm giving it all to You!)

I'm feeling. . .

....
....
....
....

I need Your help focusing my thoughts on. . .

....
....
....

Instead of ....

....
....
....

I need Your guidance with. . .

....

....

....

....

....

....

Help me to be thankful for all of life's blessings (big and small!), including. . .

....

....

....

....

....

Thank You, Father, for hearing my prayers. Amen.

They should seek God, in the hope that they might feel after Him and find Him, although He is not far from each one of us. For in Him we live and move and have our being.
ACTS 17:27–28 AMPC

DATE:

Dear Heavenly Father,

Today I am stressed because...

....

....

....

....

.... (and I'm giving it all to you!)

I'm feeling...

....

....

....

....

I need your help focusing my thoughts on...

....

....

instead of..

....

....

....

I need Your guidance with. . .

....

....

....

....

....

....

Help me to be thankful for all of life's
blessings (big and small!), including. . .

....

....

....

....

....

Thank You, Father, for hearing my prayers. Amen.

*He drew me up out of a horrible pit [a pit of
tumult and of destruction], out of the miry clay
(froth and slime), and set my feet upon a rock,
steadying my steps and establishing my goings.*

PSALM 40:2 AMPC

date:

Dear Heavenly Father,

Today I am stressed because...

....

....

....

....

.... (and I'm giving it all to you!)

I'm feeling...

....

....

....

....

I need your help focusing my thoughts on...

....

....

....

instead of ....

....

....

....

I need Your guidance with. . .

....

....

....

....

....

....

Help me to be thankful for all of life's blessings (big and small!), including. . .

....

....

....

....

....

Thank You, Father, for hearing my prayers. Amen.

God met me more than halfway, he freed me from my anxious fears. Look at him; give him your warmest smile. Never hide your feelings from him. When I was desperate, I called out, and God got me out of a tight spot.

Psalm 34:4–6 msg

Date:

Dear Heavenly Father,

Today I am stressed because. . .

....

....

....

....

.... (and I'm giving it all to you!)

I'm feeling. . .

....

....

....

....

I need your help focusing my thoughts on. . .

....

....

....

Instead of ....

....

....

....

I need Your guidance with...

....

....

....

....

Help me to be thankful for all of life's blessings (big and small!), including...

....

....

....

....

Thank You, Father, for hearing my prayers. Amen.

> God's angel sets up a circle of protection around us while we pray. Open your mouth and taste, open your eyes and see—how good God is. Blessed are you who run to him. Worship God if you want the best; worship opens doors to all his goodness.
>
> PSALM 34:7–9 MSG

DATE:

Dear Heavenly Father,

Today I am stressed because. . .

....
....
....
....
.... (and I'm giving it all to You!)

I'm feeling. . .

....
....
....
....

I need Your help focusing my thoughts on. . .

....
....
....

instead of ....

....
....
....

I need Your guidance with. . .

....

....

....

....

....

....

Help me to be thankful for all of life's blessings (big and small!), including. . .

....

....

....

....

....

Thank You, Father, for hearing my prayers. Amen.

Is anyone crying for help? GOD is listening, ready to rescue you. If your heart is broken, you'll find GOD right there; if you're kicked in the gut, he'll help you catch your breath. . . . GOD is there every time.

PSALM 34:17–19 MSG

DATE: _____

Dear Heavenly Father,

TODAY I am stressed because...

....

....

....

....

.... (and I'm giving it all to you!)

I'm feeling...

....

....

....

....

I need your help focusing my thoughts on...

....

....

....

instead of ....

....

....

....

I need Your guidance with. . .

....

....

....

....

....

....

Help me to be thankful for all of life's blessings (big and small!), including. . .

....

....

....

....

....

Thank You, Father, for hearing my prayers. Amen.

I give you thanks, O LORD, with my whole heart. . . .
On the day I called, you answered me;
my strength of soul you increased.

PSALM 138:1, 3 ESV

Date:

Dear Heavenly Father,

Today I am stressed because. . .

....
....
....
....
.... (and I'm giving it all to you!)

I'm feeling. . .

....
....
....
....

I need your help focusing my thoughts on. . .

....
....
....

instead of ....

....
....
....

I need Your guidance with. . .

....

....

....

....

....

Help me to be thankful for all of life's blessings (big and small!), including. . .

....

....

....

....

....

Thank You, Father, for hearing my prayers. Amen.

This is my prayer. That God. . .will give you spiritual wisdom and the insight to know more of him: that you may receive that inner illumination of the spirit which will make you realise how great is the hope to which he is calling you. . .and how tremendous is the power available to us who believe in God.

EPHESIANS 1:17–19 PHILLIPS

Date:

Dear Heavenly Father,

Today I am stressed because...

....

....

....

....

.... (and I'm giving it all to You!)

I'm feeling...

....

....

....

....

I need Your help focusing my thoughts on...

....

....

....

instead of ....

....

....

....

I need Your guidance with. . .

....

....

....

....

....

....

Help me to be thankful for all of life's blessings (big and small!), including. . .

....

....

....

....

....

Thank You, Father, for hearing my prayers. Amen.

God did not give us a spirit of timidity (of cowardice, of craven and cringing and fawning fear), but [He has given us a spirit] of power and of love and of calm and well-balanced mind and discipline and self-control.

2 TIMOTHY 1:7 AMPC

Date:

Dear Heavenly Father,

Today I am stressed because...

....
....
....

....

.... (and I'm giving it all to you!)

I'm feeling...

....
....
....
....

I need your help focusing my thoughts on...

....
....

instead of ....

....
....
....

I need Your guidance with. . .

....

....

....

....

....

Help me to be thankful for all of life's blessings (big and small!), including. . .

....

....

....

....

Thank You, Father, for hearing my prayers. Amen.

"May GOD, our very own God. . .keep us centered and devoted to him, following the life path he has cleared, watching the signposts, walking at the pace and rhythms he laid down for our ancestors."

1 KINGS 8:57–58 MSG

DATE:

Dear Heavenly Father,

Today I am stressed because. . .

....
....
....
....
.... (and I'm giving it all to You!)

I'm feeling. . .

....
....
....
....

I need Your help focusing my thoughts on. . .

....
....
....

instead of...
....
....
....

I need Your guidance with. . .

....

....

....

....

....

....

Help me to be thankful for all of life's blessings (big and small!), including. . .

....

....

....

....

....

Thank You, Father, for hearing my prayers. Amen.

*Now ask and keep on asking and you will receive,
so that your joy (gladness, delight)
may be full and complete.*

JOHN 16:24 AMPC

Date:

Dear Heavenly Father,

Today I am stressed because. . .

....
....
....
....
.... (and I'm giving it all to you!)

I'm feeling. . .

....
....
....
....

I need your help focusing my thoughts on. . .

....
....
....

instead of ....
....
....
....

I need Your guidance with...

....

....

....

....

....

....

Help me to be thankful for all of life's blessings (big and small!), including. . .

....

....

....

....

....

Thank You, Father, for hearing my prayers. Amen.

"So don't worry and don't keep saying, 'What shall we eat...drink or...wear?' ... Set your heart on the kingdom and his goodness, and all these things will come to you as a matter of course."
MATTHEW 6:31, 33 PHILLIPS

date:

Dear Heavenly Father,

today I am stressed because...

....

....

....

....

.... (and I'm giving it all to you!)

I'm feeling...

....

....

....

....

I need your help focusing my thoughts on...

....

....

instead of ....

....

....

I need Your guidance with. . .

....

....

....

....

....

....

Help me to be thankful for all of life's blessings (big and small!), including. . .

....

....

....

....

....

Thank You, Father, for hearing my prayers. Amen.

Throw off your old sinful nature and your former way of life, which is corrupted by lust and deception. Instead, let the Spirit renew your thoughts and attitudes. Put on your new nature, created to be like God—truly righteous and holy.

EPHESIANS 4:22–24 NLT

📅 Date:

Dear Heavenly Father,

Today I am stressed because. . .

....
....
....
....
.... (and I'm giving it all to you!)

I'm feeling. . .
....
....
....
....

I need your help focusing my thoughts on. . .
....
....
....

Instead of...
....
....
....

I need Your guidance with. . .

....

....

....

....

....

Help me to be thankful for all of life's blessings (big and small), including. . .

....

....

....

....

....

Thank You, Father, for hearing my prayers. Amen.

My child, pay attention to what I say. Listen carefully to my words. Don't lose sight of them. Let them penetrate deep into your heart, for they bring life to those who find them, and healing to their whole body.
PROVERBS 4:20–22 NLT

Date:

Dear Heavenly Father,

Today I am stressed because...

....

....

....

....

.... (and I'm giving it all to you!)

I'm feeling...

....

....

....

....

I need your help focusing my thoughts on...

....

....

....

instead of...

....

....

....

I need Your guidance with. . .

....
....
....
....
....
....

Help me to be thankful for all of life's
blessings (big and small!), including. . .

....
....
....
....
....

Thank You, Father, for hearing my prayers. Amen.

*In quietness and in [trusting]
confidence shall be your strength.*
ISAIAH 30:15 AMPC

Date:

Dear Heavenly Father,

Today I am stressed because. . .

....
....
....
....
.... (and I'm giving it all to You!)

I'm feeling. . .

....
....
....
....

I need Your help focusing my thoughts on. . .

....
....
....

Instead of ....
....
....
....

I need Your guidance with...

....

....

....

....

....

Help me to be thankful for all of life's blessings (big and small), including...

....

....

....

....

....

Thank You, Father, for hearing my prayers. Amen.

Be careful how you live.... Make the most of every opportunity.... Don't act thoughtlessly, but understand what the Lord wants you to do.... Be filled with the Holy Spirit...making music to the Lord in your hearts.
EPHESIANS 5:15–19 NLT

Dear Heavenly Father,

Today I am stressed because. . .

....
....
....
....
....

(and I'm giving it all to you!)

I'm feeling. . .

....
....
....
....

I need your help focusing my thoughts on. . .

....
....
....

instead of ....

....
....
....

I need Your guidance with. . .

....
....
....
....
....
....

Help me to be thankful for all of life's
blessings (big and small!), including. . .

....
....
....
....
....

Thank You, Father, for hearing my prayers. Amen.

"Come to me. Get away with me and you'll recover
your life. I'll show you how to take a real rest.
Walk with me and work with me—watch how
I do it. Learn the unforced rhythms of grace."
MATTHEW 11:28–30 MSG

Date:

Dear Heavenly Father,

Today I am stressed because...

(and I'm giving it all to You!)

I'm feeling...

I need Your help focusing my thoughts on...

instead of

I need Your guidance with. . .

....

....

....

....

....

Help me to be thankful for all of life's blessings (big and small!), including. . .

....

....

....

....

....

Thank You, Father, for hearing my prayers. Amen.

Let petitions and praises shape your worries into prayers, letting God know your concerns. Before you know it, a sense of God's wholeness, everything coming together for good, will come and settle you down. It's wonderful what happens when Christ displaces worry at the center of your life.

PHILIPPIANS 4:6–7 MSG

DATE:

Dear Heavenly Father,

today I am stressed because...

....
....
....
....
.... (and I'm giving it all to you!)

I'm feeling...

....
....
....
....

I need your help focusing my thoughts on...

....
....

instead of ....
....
....
....

I need Your guidance with...

....

....

....

....

....

Help me to be thankful for all of life's
blessings (big and small!), including...

....

....

....

....

Thank You, Father, for hearing my prayers. Amen.

In peace I will both lie down and sleep, for You, Lord,
alone make me dwell in safety and confident trust.
PSALM 4:8 AMPC

DATE:

Dear Heavenly Father,

TODAY I AM STRESSED because...

....

....

....

....

.... (AND I'M GIVING IT ALL TO YOU!)

I'm feeling...

....

....

....

....

I need your help focusing my thoughts on...

....

....

....

instead of ....

....

....

....

I need Your guidance with. . .

....

....

....

....

....

....

Help me to be thankful for all of life's
blessings (big and small!), including. . .

....

....

....

....

....

Thank You, Father, for hearing my prayers. Amen.

"For my thoughts are not your thoughts, neither are your
ways my ways, declares the LORD. For as the heavens are
higher than the earth, so are my ways higher than
your ways and my thoughts than your thoughts."
ISAIAH 55:8–9 ESV

DATE:

Dear Heavenly Father,

Today I am stressed because. . .

....
....
....
....
....

.... (and I'm giving it all to You!)

I'm feeling. . .

....
....
....
....

I need Your help focusing my thoughts on. . .

....
....
....

instead of ....

....
....
....

I need Your guidance with. . .

....

....

....

....

....

....

Help me to be thankful for all of life's blessings (big and small!), including. . .

....

....

....

....

Thank You, Father, for hearing my prayers. Amen.

"Embrace this God-life. . .and nothing will be too much for you. This mountain, for instance: Just say, 'Go jump in the lake'—no shuffling or shilly-shallying— and it's as good as done. That's why I urge you to pray for absolutely everything."

MARK 11:23–24 MSG

DATE:

Dear Heavenly Father,

Today I am stressed because...

....
....
....
....
.... (and I'm giving it all to you!)

I'm feeling...

....
....
....
....

I need your help focusing my thoughts on...

....
....
....

instead of...
....
....
....

I need Your guidance with. . .

....

....

....

....

....

....

Help me to be thankful for all of life's blessings (big and small!), including. . .

....

....

....

....

....

Thank You, Father, for hearing my prayers. Amen.

*Sing GOD a brand-new song! Earth and everyone
in it, sing! Sing to GOD—worship GOD!*
PSALM 96:1 MSG

Date:

Dear Heavenly Father,

Today I am stressed because...

....
....
....
....
.... (and I'm giving it all to You!)

I'm feeling...

....
....
....
....

I need Your help focusing my thoughts on...

....
....
....

instead of ....

....
....
....

I need Your guidance with. . .

....

....

....

....

....

Help me to be thankful for all of life's blessings (big and small!), including. . .

....

....

....

....

....

Thank You, Father, for hearing my prayers. Amen.

I have strength for all things in Christ Who empowers me [I am ready for anything and equal to anything through Him Who infuses inner strength into me; I am self-sufficient in Christ's sufficiency].
PHILIPPIANS 4:13 AMPC

DATE:

Dear Heavenly Father,

today I am stressed because. . .

....
....
....
....
.... (and I'm giving it all to you!)

I'm feeling. . .

....
....
....
....

I need your help focusing my thoughts on. . .

....
....
....

instead of ....
....
....
....

I need Your guidance with. . .

....

....

....

....

....

Help me to be thankful for all of life's blessings (big and small!), including. . .

....

....

....

....

....

Thank You, Father, for hearing my prayers. Amen.

Clothe yourselves with tenderhearted mercy, kindness, humility, gentleness, and patience. Make allowance for each other's faults, and forgive anyone who offends you. Remember, the Lord forgave you, so you must forgive others.

COLOSSIANS 3:12–13 NLT

DATE:

Dear Heavenly Father,

Today I am stressed because. . .

....

....

....

....

.... (and I'm giving it all to you!)

I'm feeling. . .

....

....

....

....

I need your help focusing my thoughts on. . .

....

....

....

instead of ....

....

....

....

I need Your guidance with. . .

....

....

....

....

....

....

Help me to be thankful for all of life's blessings (big and small), including. . .

....

....

....

....

....

Thank You, Father, for hearing my prayers. Amen.

[What, what would have become of me] had I not believed that I would see the Lord's goodness in the land of the living! Wait and hope for and expect the Lord; be brave and of good courage and let your heart be stout and enduring.

PSALM 27:13–14 AMPC

Date:

Dear Heavenly Father,

Today I am stressed because...

....
....
....
....
.... (and I'm giving it all to you!)

I'm feeling...

....
....
....
....

I need your help focusing my thoughts on...

....
....
....

instead of ....
....
....
....

I need Your guidance with...

....

....

....

....

....

Help me to be thankful for all of life's blessings (big and small!), including...

....

....

....

....

Thank You, Father, for hearing my prayers. Amen.

Trust (lean on, rely on, and be confident) in the Lord and do good; so shall you dwell in the land and feed surely on His faithfulness, and truly you shall be fed.

PSALM 37:3 AMPC

DATE: _____

Dear Heavenly Father,

TODAY I am stressed because...

....
....
....
....
.... (and I'm giving it all to you!)

I'm feeling...

....
....
....
....

I need your help focusing my thoughts on...

....
....
....

instead of...
....
....
....

I need Your guidance with. . .

....
....
....
....
....
....

Help me to be thankful for all of life's blessings (big and small!), including. . .

....
....
....
....
....

Thank You, Father, for hearing my prayers. Amen.

Delight yourself also in the Lord, and He will give you the desires and secret petitions of your heart.

PSALM 37:4 AMPC

Date:

Dear Heavenly Father,

today I am stressed because...

....

....

....

....

.... (and I'm giving it all to you!)

I'm feeling...

....

....

....

....

I need your help focusing my thoughts on...

....

....

....

instead of ....

....

....

....

I need Your guidance with. . .

....

....

....

....

....

....

Help me to be thankful for all of life's blessings (big and small!), including. . .

....

....

....

....

....

Thank You, Father, for hearing my prayers. Amen.

Commit your way to the Lord [roll and repose each care of your load on Him]; trust (lean on, rely on, and be confident) also in Him and He will bring it to pass.
PSALM 37:5 AMPC

DATE:

Dear Heavenly Father,

Today I am stressed because. . .

....

....

....

....

.... (and I'm giving it all to you!)

I'm feeling. . .

....

....

....

....

I need your help focusing my thoughts on. . .

....

....

instead of ....

....

....

....

I need Your guidance with. . .

....

....

....

....

....

Help me to be thankful for all of life's blessings (big and small!), including. . .

....

....

....

....

Thank You, Father, for hearing my prayers. Amen.

Be still and rest in the Lord; wait for Him and patiently lean yourself upon Him; fret not yourself because of him who prospers in his way.

PSALM 37:7 AMPC

date:

Dear Heavenly Father,

Today I am stressed because...

....

....

....

....

.... (and I'm giving it all to you!)

I'm feeling...

....

....

....

....

I need your help focusing my thoughts on...

....

....

instead of ....

....

....

....

I need Your guidance with. . .

....

....

....

....

....

....

Help me to be thankful for all of life's
blessings (big and small!), including. . .

....

....

....

....

....

Thank You, Father, for hearing my prayers. Amen.

*When I am afraid, I put my trust in you. In God, whose
word I praise, in God I trust; I shall not be afraid. . . .
This I know, that God is for me. In God, whose word
I praise, in the LORD, whose word I praise,
in God I trust; I shall not be afraid.*

PSALM 56:3–4, 9–11 ESV

Date:

Dear Heavenly Father,

Today I am stressed because. . .

....

....

....

....

.... (and I'm giving it all to You!)

I'm feeling. . .

....

....

....

....

I need Your help focusing my thoughts on. . .

....

....

....

instead of ....

....

....

....

I need Your guidance with...

....
....
....
....
....
....

Help me to be thankful for all of life's blessings (big and small!), including. . .

....
....
....
....
....

Thank You, Father, for hearing my prayers. Amen.

This is the day that the LORD has made;
let us rejoice and be glad in it.
PSALM 118:24 ESV

Date:

Dear Heavenly Father, . . .

Today I am stressed because. . .

....

....

....

....

.... (and I'm giving it all to You!)

I'm feeling. . .

....

....

....

....

I need Your help focusing my thoughts on. . .

....

....

....

instead of ....

....

....

....

I need Your guidance with. . .

....

....

....

....

....

....

HeLP me to be thankful for all of life's
blessings (big and small!), including. . .

....

....

....

....

....

Thank You, Father, for hearing my prayers. Amen.

*The name of the Lord is a strong tower; the
[consistently] righteous man [upright and in
right standing with God] runs into it and is
safe, high [above evil] and strong.*

PROVERBS 18:10 AMPC

DATE:

Dear Heavenly Father,

Today I am stressed because. . .

....
....
....
....
.... (and I'm giving it all to You!)

I'm feeling. . .

....
....
....
....

I need Your help focusing my thoughts on. . .

....
....
....
instead of...
....
....
....

I need Your guidance with. . .

....
....
....
....
....
....

Help me to be thankful for all of life's blessings (big and small), including. . .

....
....
....
....
....

Thank You, Father, for hearing my prayers. Amen.

Cast your burden on the Lord [releasing the weight of it] and He will sustain you; He will never allow the [consistently] righteous to be moved (made to slip, fall, or fail).
PSALM 55:22 AMPC

DATE:

Dear Heavenly Father,

Today I am stressed because. . .

....
....
....
....
.... (and I'm giving it all to You!)

I'm feeling. . .

....
....
....
....

I need Your help focusing my thoughts on. . .

....
....
....

instead of ....

....
....
....

I need Your guidance with. . .

....

....

....

....

....

....

Help me to be thankful for all of life's blessings (big and small!), including. . .

....

....

....

....

....

Thank You, Father, for hearing my prayers. Amen.

The God of heaven. . .gives wisdom to the wise and knowledge to those who have understanding! He reveals the deep and secret things; He knows what is in the darkness, and the light dwells with Him!

DANIEL 2:19, 21–22 AMPC

DATE:

Dear Heavenly Father,

Today I am stressed because...

....
....
....
....
.... (and I'm giving it all to You!)

I'm feeling...

....
....
....
....

I need your help focusing my thoughts on...

....
....

instead of ....

....
....
....

I need Your guidance with...

....

....

....

....

....

....

Help me to be thankful for all of life's
blessings (big and small!), including...

....

....

....

....

....

Thank You, Father, for hearing my prayers. Amen.

*In my distress I cried out to the LORD; yes, I prayed to my
God for help. He heard me from his sanctuary; my cry to
him reached his ears.... He reached down from heaven
and rescued me; he drew me out of deep waters.*

PSALM 18:6, 16 NLT

Date:

Dear Heavenly Father,

Today I am stressed because...

....

....

....

....

.... (and I'm giving it all to You!)

I'm feeling...

....

....

....

....

I need Your help focusing my thoughts on...

....

....

instead of ....

....

....

....

I need Your guidance with. . .

....

....

....

....

....

Help me to be thankful for all of life's blessings (big and small!), including. . .

....

....

....

....

....

Thank You, Father, for hearing my prayers. Amen.

Carefully build yourselves up in this most holy faith by praying in the Holy Spirit, staying right at the center of God's love, keeping your arms open and outstretched, ready for the mercy of our Master, Jesus Christ. This is the unending life, the real life!

JUDE 1:20–21 MSG

Date:

Dear Heavenly Father,

Today I am stressed because. . .

....

....

....

....

.... (and I'm giving it all to you!)

I'm feeling. . .

....

....

....

....

I need your help focusing my thoughts on. . .

....

....

....

instead of ....

....

....

....

I need Your guidance with. . .

....

....

....

....

....

Help me to be thankful for all of life's blessings (big and small!), including. . .

....

....

....

....

Thank You, Father, for hearing my prayers. Amen.

"This is GOD's Message, the God who made earth, made it livable and lasting, known everywhere as GOD: 'Call to me and I will answer you. I'll tell you marvelous and wondrous things that you could never figure out on your own.'"
JEREMIAH 33:3 MSG

Date:

Dear Heavenly Father,

Today I am stressed because. . .

....

....

....

....

.... (and I'm giving it all to you!)

I'm feeling. . .

....

....

....

....

I need your help focusing my thoughts on. . .

....

....

....

instead of..

....

....

....

I need Your guidance with. . .

....

....

....

....

....

....

Help me to be thankful for all of life's
blessings (big and small!), including. . .

....

....

....

....

....

Thank You, Father, for hearing my prayers. Amen.

"When two of you get together on anything
at all on earth and make a prayer of it, my
Father in heaven goes into action. And when
two or three of you are together because of
me, you can be sure that I'll be there."

MATTHEW 18:20 MSG

DATE:

Dear Heavenly Father,

Today I am stressed because...

....

....

....

....

.... (and I'm giving it all to you!)

I'm feeling...

....

....

....

....

I need your help focusing my thoughts on...

....

....

....

instead of ....

....

....

....

I need Your guidance with. . .

....

....

....

....

....

....

Help me to be thankful for all of life's blessings (big and small!), including. . .

....

....

....

....

....

Thank You, Father, for hearing my prayers. Amen.

*Therefore we do not become discouraged (utterly
spiritless, exhausted, and wearied out through fear).
Though our outer man is [progressively] decaying
and wasting away, yet our inner self is being
[progressively] renewed day after day.*
2 Corinthians 4:16 ampc

Date:

Dear Heavenly Father,

Today I am stressed because...

....

....

....

....

.... (and I'm giving it all to You!)

I'm feeling...

....

....

....

....

I need Your help focusing my thoughts on...

....

....

instead of ....

....

....

....

I need Your guidance with...

....

....

....

....

....

....

Help me to be thankful for all of life's blessings (big and small), including. . .

....

....

....

....

....

Thank You, Father, for hearing my prayers. Amen.

"With him is an arm of flesh, but with us is the LORD our God, to help us and to fight our battles."
2 CHRONICLES 32:8 ESV

DATE:

Dear Heavenly Father,

Today I am stressed because. . .

....

....

....

....

.... (and I'm giving it all to you!)

I'm feeling. . .

....

....

....

....

I need your help focusing my thoughts on. . .

....

....

....

instead of ....

....

....

....

I need Your guidance with. . .

....

....

....

....

....

....

Help me to be thankful for all of life's blessings (big and small!), including. . .

....

....

....

....

....

Thank You, Father, for hearing my prayers. Amen.

If we live by the [Holy] Spirit, let us also walk by the Spirit. [If by the Holy Spirit we have our life in God, let us go forward walking in line, our conduct controlled by the Spirit.]
Galatians 5:25 ampc

DATE:

Dear Heavenly Father,

Today I am stressed because. . .

....
....
....
....
.... (and I'm giving it all to You!)

I'm feeling. . .

....
....
....
....

I need your help focusing my thoughts on. . .

....
....

instead of ....
....
....
....

I need Your guidance with. . .

....

....

....

....

....

....

Help me to be thankful for all of life's
blessings (big and small), including. . .

....

....

....

....

....

Thank You, Father, for hearing my prayers. Amen.

*We're depending on GOD; he's everything we need.
What's more, our hearts brim with joy since we've
taken for our own his holy name. Love us, GOD,
with all you've got—that's what we're depending on.*
PSALM 33:20–21 MSG

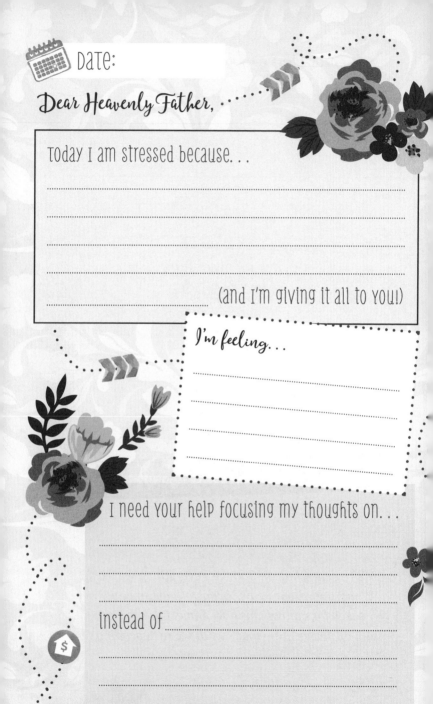

Date:

Dear Heavenly Father,

Today I am stressed because...

....

....

....

....

.... (and I'm giving it all to you!)

I'm feeling...

....

....

....

....

I need your help focusing my thoughts on...

....

....

....

instead of ....

....

....

....

I need Your guidance with. . .

....

....

....

....

....

Help me to be thankful for all of life's
blessings (big and small!), including. . .

....

....

....

....

Thank You, Father, for hearing my prayers. Amen.

*If you seek Him [inquiring for and of Him,
craving Him as your soul's first necessity],
He will be found by you.*

2 CHRONICLES 15:2 AMPC

Date:

Dear Heavenly Father,

Today I am stressed because...

....
....
....
....
.... (and I'm giving it all to you!)

I'm feeling...

....
....
....
....

I need your help focusing my thoughts on...

....
....
....

Instead of ....
....
....
....

I need Your guidance with. . .

....

....

....

....

....

....

Help me to be thankful for all of life's blessings (big and small!), including. . .

....

....

....

....

....

Thank You, Father, for hearing my prayers. Amen.

The Holy Spirit helps us in our weakness.
For example, we don't know what God wants us
to pray for. But the Holy Spirit prays for us with
groanings that cannot be expressed in words.
ROMANS 8:26 NLT

Date:

Dear Heavenly Father,

Today I am stressed because. . .

....
....
....
....
.... (and I'm giving it all to you!)

I'm feeling. . .

....
....
....
....

I need your help focusing my thoughts on. . .

....
....
....

instead of ....
....
....
....

I need Your guidance with. . .

....

....

....

....

....

Help me to be thankful for all of life's
blessings (big and small!), including. . .

....

....

....

....

....

Thank You, Father, for hearing my prayers. Amen.

*O God. . .I will hide beneath the shadow of your
wings until the danger passes by. I cry out to God
Most High. . .who will fulfill his purpose for me.
He will send help from heaven to rescue me.*

PSALM 57:1–3 NLT

Date:

Dear Heavenly Father,

Today I am stressed because. . .

....

....

....

....

.... (and I'm giving it all to you!)

I'm feeling. . .

....

....

....

....

I need your help focusing my thoughts on. . .

....

....

....

instead of ....

....

....

....

I need Your guidance with. . .

....

....

....

....

....

Help me to be thankful for all of life's blessings (big and small!), including. . .

....

....

....

....

....

Thank You, Father, for hearing my prayers. Amen.

*My heart is confident in you, O God. . . . No wonder
I can sing your praises! Wake up, my heart! Wake
up, O lyre and harp! I will wake the dawn with
my song. . . . I will sing your praises. . . . For your
unfailing love is as high as the heavens.*
PSALM 57:7–10 NLT

DATE:

Dear Heavenly Father,

TODAY I AM STRESSED BECAUSE. . .

....
....
....
....
.... (and I'm giving it all to you!)

I'm feeling. . .

....
....
....
....

I NEED YOUR HELP FOCUSING MY THOUGHTS ON. . .

....
....
....

instead of..
....
....
....

I need Your guidance with...

....

....

....

....

....

....

Help me to be thankful for all of life's blessings (big and small!), including. . .

....

....

....

....

....

Thank You, Father, for hearing my prayers. Amen.

Delight yourselves in God, yes, find your joy in him at all times. Have a reputation for gentleness, and never forget the nearness of your Lord.

PHILIPPIANS 4:4–5 PHILLIPS

DATE:

Dear Heavenly Father,

Today I am stressed because. . .

....

....

....

....

.... (and I'm giving it all to you!)

I'm feeling. . .

....

....

....

....

I need your help focusing my thoughts on. . .

....

....

....

instead of ....

....

....

....

I need Your guidance with. . .

....

....

....

....

....

Help me to be thankful for all of life's blessings (big and small), including. . .

....

....

....

....

....

Thank You, Father, for hearing my prayers. Amen.

I have learned to be content, whatever the circumstances may be. I know now how to live when things are difficult and I know how to live when things are prosperous. In general and in particular I have learned the secret of facing either poverty or plenty.

PHILIPPIANS 4:11–12 PHILLIPS

DATE:

Dear Heavenly Father,

today I am stressed because...

....

....

....

....

.... (and I'm giving it all to you!)

I'm feeling...

....

....

....

....

I need your help focusing my thoughts on...

....

....

....

instead of ....

....

....

....

I need Your guidance with. . .

....

....

....

....

....

....

Help me to be thankful for all of life's blessings (big and small), including. . .

....

....

....

....

....

Thank You, Father, for hearing my prayers. Amen.

We can be full of joy here and now even in our trials and troubles. Taken in the right spirit these very things will give us patient endurance; this in turn will develop a mature character, and a character of this sort produces a steady hope, a hope that will never disappoint us.

ROMANS 5:3–4 PHILLIPS

DATE:

Dear Heavenly Father,

Today I am stressed because...

....

....

....

....

.... (and I'm giving it all to you!)

I'm feeling...

....

....

....

....

I need your help focusing my thoughts on...

....

....

....

instead of ....

....

....

....

I need Your guidance with. . .

....

....

....

....

....

....

Help me to be thankful for all of life's blessings (big and small!), including. . .

....

....

....

....

....

Thank You, Father, for hearing my prayers. Amen.

But he's already made it plain how to live, what to do, what GOD is looking for in. . .women. It's quite simple: Do what is fair and just to your neighbor, be compassionate and loyal in your love, and don't take yourself too seriously—take God seriously.

MICAH 6:8 MSG

DATE:

Dear Heavenly Father,

Today I am stressed because. . .

....
....
....
....
.... (and I'm giving it all to you!)

I'm feeling. . .

....
....
....
....

I need your help focusing my thoughts on. . .

....
....
....

Instead of ....
....
....
....

I need Your guidance with. . .

_____
_____
_____
_____
_____
_____

Help me to be thankful for all of life's blessings (big and small!), including. . .

....
....
....
....
....

Thank You, Father, for hearing my prayers. Amen.

Now all glory to God, who is able, through his mighty power at work within us, to accomplish infinitely more than we might ask or think.
EPHESIANS 3:20 NLT

Dear Heavenly Father,

Today I am stressed because. . .

....

....

....

....

.... (and I'm giving it all to you!)

I'm feeling. . .

....

....

....

....

I need your help focusing my thoughts on. . .

....

....

instead of...

....

....

I need Your guidance with. . .

....
....
....
....
....

Help me to be thankful for all of life's blessings (big and small!), including. . .

....
....
....
....
....

Thank You, Father, for hearing my prayers. Amen.

For his unfailing love toward those who fear him is as great as the height of the heavens above the earth. He has removed our sins as far from us as the east is from the west.
PSALM 103:11–12 NLT

DATE:

Dear Heavenly Father,

Today I am stressed because. . .

....

....

....

....

.... (and I'm giving it all to you!)

I'm feeling. . .

....

....

....

....

I need your help focusing my thoughts on. . .

....

....

instead of ....

....

....

....

I need Your guidance with. . .

....
....
....
....
....
....

Help me to be thankful for all of life's blessings (big and small!), including. . .

....
....
....
....
....

Thank You, Father, for hearing my prayers. Amen.

So humble yourselves under the mighty power of God, and at the right time he will lift you up in honor. Give all your worries and cares to God, for he cares about you.

1 Peter 5:6–7 nlt

date:

Dear Heavenly Father,

Today I am stressed because. . .

....

....

....

....

.... (and I'm giving it all to you!)

I'm feeling. . .

....

....

....

....

I need your help focusing my thoughts on. . .

....

....

....

instead of ....

....

....

....

I need Your guidance with. . .

....

....

....

....

....

Help me to be thankful for all of life's blessings (big and small!), including. . .

....

....

....

....

....

Thank You, Father, for hearing my prayers. Amen.

God means what he says. What he says goes. His powerful Word is sharp as a surgeon's scalpel, cutting through everything, whether doubt or defense, laying us open to listen and obey.

HEBREWS 4:12 MSG

Date:

Dear Heavenly Father,

Today I am stressed because. . .

....

....

....

....

.... (and I'm giving it all to you!)

I'm feeling. . .

....

....

....

....

I need your help focusing my thoughts on. . .

....

....

....

instead of ....

....

....

....

I need Your guidance with. . .

....

....

....

....

....

....

Help me to be thankful for all of life's blessings (big and small!), including. . .

....

....

....

....

....

Thank You, Father, for hearing my prayers. Amen.

*Behold, I stand at the door and knock; if anyone
hears and listens to and heeds My voice and
opens the door, I will come in to him.*

REVELATION 3:20 AMPC

Discover More Faith Maps for the Entire Family...

The Prayer Map for Men
978-1-64352-438-2

The Prayer Map for Women
978-1-68322-557-7

The Prayer Map for Girls
978-1-68322-559-1

The Prayer Map for Boys
978-1-68322-558-4

The Prayer Map for Teens
978-1-68322-556-0

These purposeful prayer journals are a fun and creative way to more fully experience the power of prayer. Each page guides you to write out thoughts, ideas, and lists...which then creates a specific "map" for you to follow as you talk to God. Each map includes a spot to record the date, so you can look back on your prayers and see how God has worked in your life. *The Prayer Map* will not only encourage you to spend time talking with God about the things that matter most...it will also help you build a healthy spiritual habit of continual prayer for life!

Spiral Bound / $7.99